Join my newsletter and get
my ebook library for FREE!

INGO BLUM

WHERE IS MY LITTLE CROCODILE?

WO IST MEIN KLEINES KROKODIL?

ENGLISH/GERMAN

4

Where is Charlie, my little crocodile?

Wo ist Charlie, mein kleines Krokodil?

He is not in the garden.

Er ist nicht im Garten.

He is not in the tree.

Er ist nicht auf dem Baum.

He cannot climb.

Er kann nicht klettern.

He is not on the street.

Er ist nicht auf der Strasse.

The street is empty.

Die Strasse ist leer.

10

He is not in the restaurant.

Er ist nicht im Restaurant.

Crocodiles are not allowed
in restaurants.

Krokodile sind in
Restaurants
nicht erlaubt.

ZOO
Monkey
12

He is not at the zoo.

Er ist nicht im Zoo.

Where is Charlie?

Wo ist Charlie?

Is he driving a car?

Fährt er mit dem Auto?

Can crocodiles drive cars?

Können Krokodile Auto
fahren?

Is he climbing the mountain?

Klettert er auf den Berg?

That is difficult for Charlie.

Das ist schwierig für Charlie.

18

Is he sleeping by the river?

Schläft er am Fluss?

That`s cozy!

Das ist gemütlich.

There he is! Hooray!
Da ist er! Hurra!

Charlie sleeps in his bed.
Charlie schläft in seinem Bett.

Good Night!
Gute Nacht!

Color the crocodile.

Mal das Krokodil aus.

More Reading and Coloring Fun

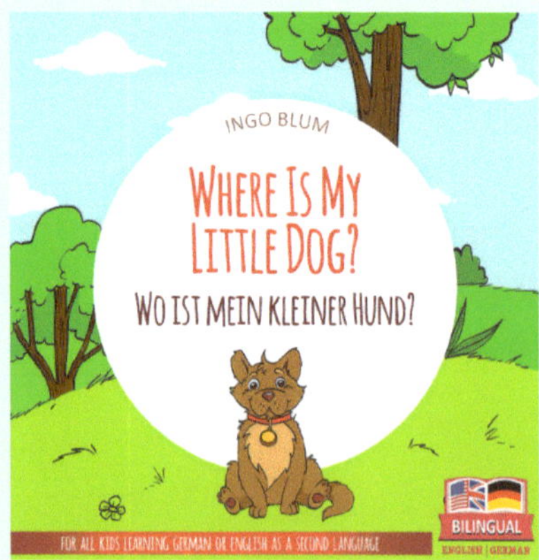

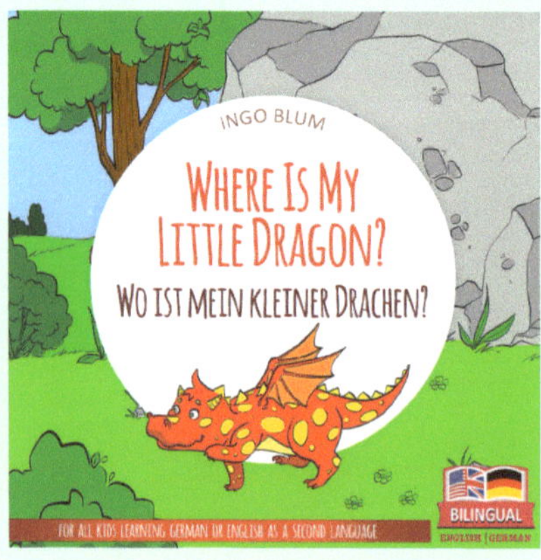

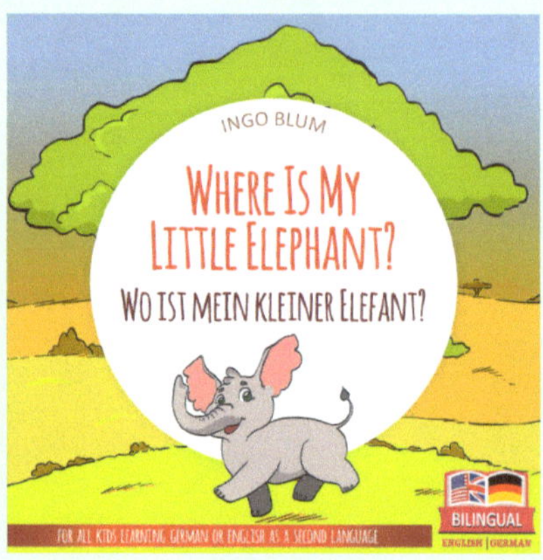

ISBN 978-1-982925-46-8   ISBN 978-1-982924-05-8   ISBN 978-1-982924-98-0

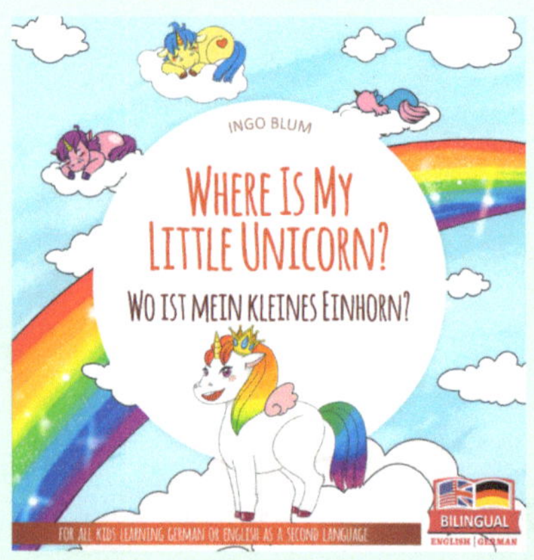

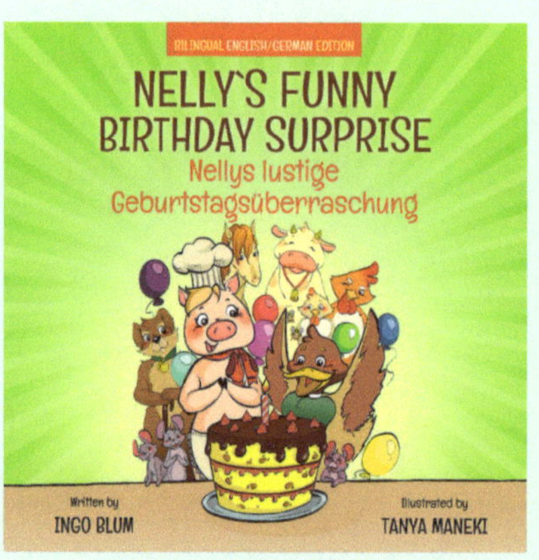

ISBN 979-8-460931-34-7   ISBN 978-1-983093-97-5   ISBN 979-8-682547-90-6

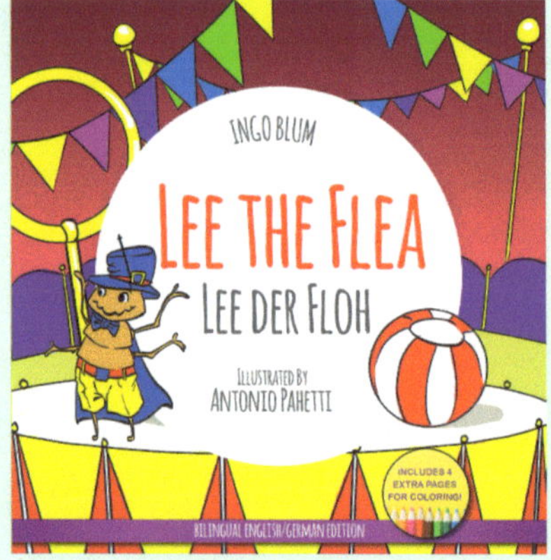

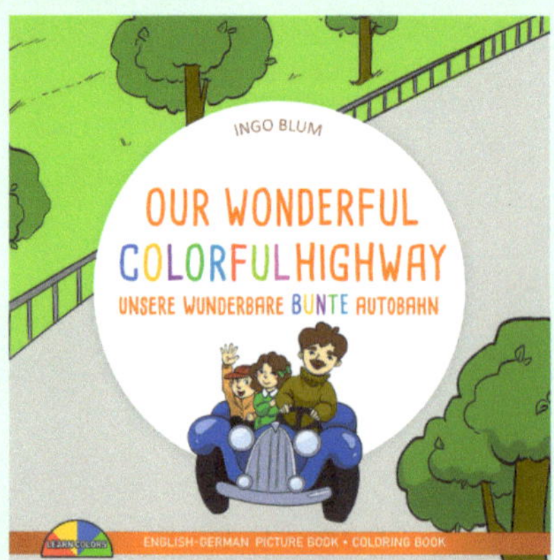

ISBN 978-1-790104-73-4   ISBN 979-8-672025-68-1   ISBN 978-1-982925-84-0